W9-BCT-076

DISCOVER

Shadows

BY PAMELA HALL • ILLUSTRATED BY JANE YAMADA

**The Child's World**®

PUBLISHED by The Child's World®
1980 Lookout Drive • Mankato, MN 56003-1705
800-599-READ • www.childsworld.com

ACKNOWLEDGMENTS

The Child's World®: Mary Berendes, Publishing Director
The Design Lab: Design
Jody Jensen Shaffer: Editing
Pamela J. Mitsakos: Photo Research

PHOTO CREDITS

© alexmak72427/Shutterstock.com: 5; Amy Johansson/Shutterstock.com:
19; Digital Media Pro/Shutterstock.com: 12; Heiko Kueverling/Shutterstock.
com: 11; JHLloyd/iStock.com: 7; Jot/iStock.com: 8; pat138241/123RF.com:
13; Pichi/Shutterstock.com: 9; Photick/Odilon Dimier/Thinkstock.com: 16;
pjmorley/iStock.com: 15; ShaneKato/iStock.com: 18; stacey_newman/iStock.
com: 17; toskov/iStock.com: cover, 1; vasiliki/iStock.com: 6

ISBN 9781626873056
LCCN 2014930657

PRINTED in the United States of America • Mankato, MN
July, 2014 • PA02220

CONTENTS

SHADOWS BIG AND SMALL

They stretch.

They shift.

They flutter and sway.

Big and small,

shadows are everywhere.

Big and small things cast shadows.

CREATING SHADOWS

On sunny days your shadow follows you around.
But on cloudy days, you're on your own. Why?
It takes bright light to make a shadow.

The sun helps make your shadow.

When the sun is hidden, you have no shadow.

Rays of light move in straight lines. Your body blocks light's path. Your body makes a dark shape on the ground—a you-shaped shadow!

Your shadow is always shaped like you!

The bicycle blocks light rays. It makes a bicycle-shaped shadow.

Ants, skyscrapers, leaves, airplanes—most things make shadows. These things block light. They are **opaque**.

But some things let light shine through. Clear glass is see-through. It doesn't make shadows.

Glass in a window doesn't make a shadow. But the frames in a window do.

BIG AND BIGGER SHADOWS

On a summer day, it feels so good to cool off in the shade.

Trees provide lots of shade on sunny days.

An umbrella at the beach makes shade.

What things make shade? Trees, buildings, and mountains can. Shade is just a big shadow.

Night is an even bigger shadow. Earth is always spinning. During the day, your side of Earth is facing the sun.

At night, your side of Earth is away from the sun. You are in Earth's shadow.

It's night in the parts of Earth that are in shadow.

CHANGING SHADOWS

Your shadow changes throughout the day. At noon, the sun is high in the sky. Your shadow is short.

What time of day does this picture show?

When the sun is rising or setting, your shadow is long.

In the morning and the evening, the sun is low. Your shadow stretches long.

Where is your shadow? It depends. When light is in front of you, your shadow falls behind.

When you face the sun, your shadow trails behind you.

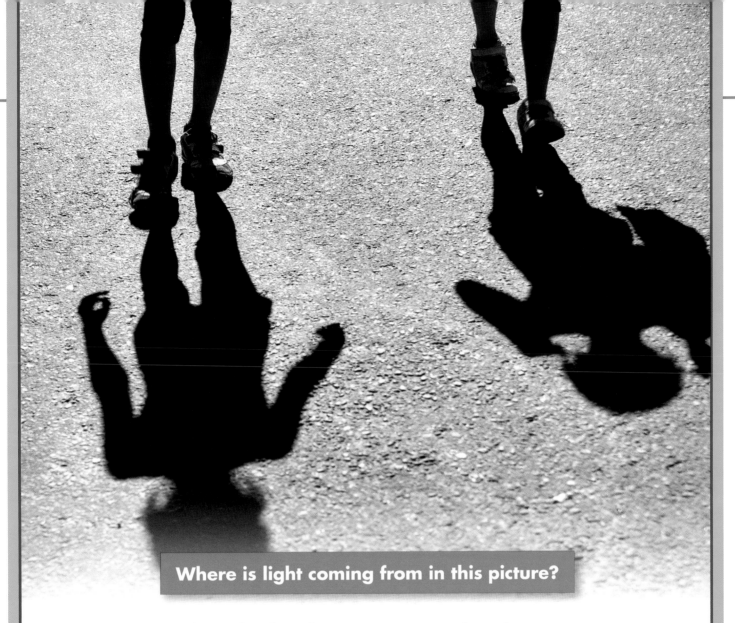

Where is light coming from in this picture?

But when light shines at your back, your
shadow goes before you.

19

SHADOW PLAY

It's time to play with shadows!

Can you make a shadow monster with your hand?

Can you fit inside your friend's shadow shape?

Make your shadow high-five your friend's shadow.

Notice all the different shadows around you.

KINDS OF SHADOWS

PALE SHADOWS	BIG SHADOWS	FUZZY SHADOWS
Some things don't block out all the light. They let some light through. They make pale shadows.	Big things make big shadows. But small things can make big shadows, too. The closer something is to the light, the bigger its shadow.	When something is far away from its shadow, its shadow is fuzzy.

GLOSSARY

cast (KAST): To cast is to make, especially when it comes to shadows. On sunny days, your body casts a shadow.

opaque (oh-PAYK): Opaque things are not see-through. By blocking light, opaque objects make shadows.

rays (RAYZ): Rays are straight lines by which light travels. Shadows are made when things block light rays.

TO LEARN MORE

In the Library

Bulla, Clyde Robert. *What Makes a Shadow?*
New York: HarperCollins, 1994.

Hoban, Tana. *Shadows and Reflections.* New
York: Greenwillow Books, 1990.

Swinburne, Stephen R. *Guess Whose Shadow?*
Honesdale, PA: Boyds Mill Press, 2002.

On the Web

Visit our Web site for lots of links about Shadows:

www.childsworld.com/links

Note to Parents, Teachers, and Librarians: We routinely check our Web links to make sure they're safe, active sites—so encourage your readers to check them out!

INDEX